BABY RECORD

THE FIRST FIVE YEARS

IMAGES BY

ANNE GEDDES

ANNE GEDDES ™

ISBN 0-7683-2024-0

© Anne Geddes 1997

Published in 1997 by Photogenique Publishers (a division of Hodder Moa Beckett)
Studio 3.16, Axis Building, 1 Cleveland Road, Parnell
Auckland, New Zealand

First USA edition published in 1997 by Cedco Publishing Company,
100 Pelican Way, San Rafael, CA 94901

Designed by Frances Young
Produced by Kel Geddes
Color separations by MH Group

Printed through Midas Printing Limited, Hong Kong

Please write to us for a FREE FULL COLOR catalog of our fine Anne Geddes
calendars and books, Cedco Publishing Company, 100 Pelican Way,
San Rafael, CA 94901.
or, visit our website : www.cedco.com

10 9 8 7 6 5 4 3 2

*A*nne Geddes is an Australian born professional photographer living in Auckland, New Zealand.

The worldwide success of her best selling book Down in the Garden continues to reinforce the title that Anne has earned of being the pre-eminent photographer of children in the world today.

Anne has said the following about her work, "I am frequently asked why I photograph babies so often, and where my ideas come from. Little babies are indeed my inspiration, and I cannot imagine a photographic life without them playing a major part in it. Where this special love for babies comes from I cannot tell you, and I have spent much time searching for an answer myself. All I know is that they are all perfect little human beings in their own ways, and we should all take the time to cherish them, especially while they are very small."

This book is intended to help you and your child cherish those unique, first five years in which so many changes and priceless moments occur.

Contents

My Birth

My Name is

_____

I was born on _____

at _____

_____

The time was _____

I was delivered by _____

_____

I weighed _____

and measured _____

My eyes were _____

My hair color was _____

Mementos

My Birth Announcement

A lock of hair

My hospital tag

Newspaper Clippings

What was happening in the world

Photographs

Comments

Mother _____

_____

_____

_____

Father _____

_____

_____

_____

Special Messages

Family _____

_____

_____

_____

_____

Friends _____

_____

_____

_____

Visitors and Gifts

Signs

Star Sign _____

_____

Chinese Year _____

_____

Birth Stone _____

_____

Birth Flower _____

_____

_____

Naming

My full name is _____

My name was chosen by _____

because _____

My pet names are _____

Ceremonies celebrating my birth _____

at _____

Comments _____

_____

_____

Photographs

My Family Tree

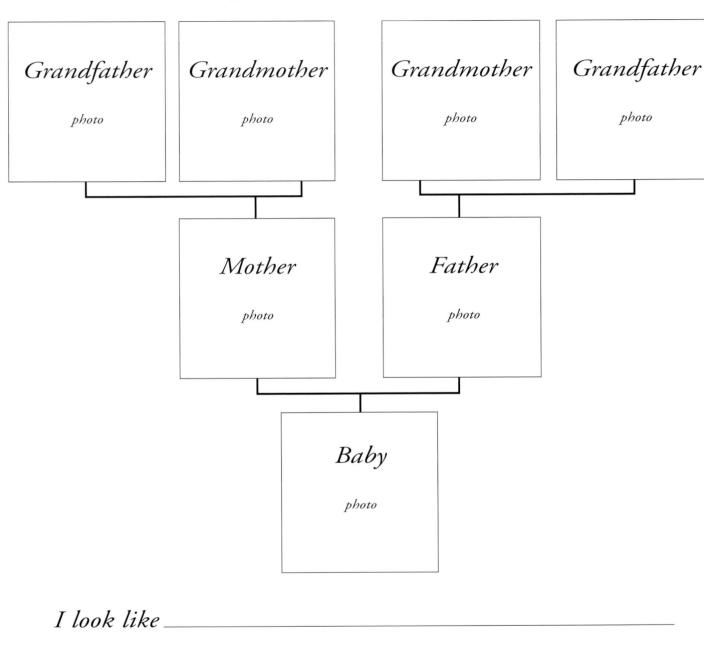

Grandfather
photo

Grandmother
photo

Grandmother
photo

Grandfather
photo

Mother
photo

Father
photo

Baby
photo

I look like _____

_____

Photographs

Brothers and Sisters

Three Months

Weight _____

Length _____

Comments _____

_____

_____

_____

_____

_____

Photographs

Six Months

Weight _____

Length _____

Comments _____

_____

_____

_____

_____

_____

Photographs

Nine Months

Weight _____

Length _____

Comments _____

_____

_____

_____

_____

_____

_____

Photographs

Milestones

I first smiled _____

laughed _____

grasped a toy _____

I held my head up _____

I slept through the night _____

rolled over _____

sat up _____

Comments _____

_____

I first crawled _____

stood up _____

walked _____

My first tooth _____

My first word _____

Comments _____

_____

_____

_____

Food

My first solid food _____

I was weaned _____

I drank from a cup _____

Finger food _____

I fed myself _____

_____

I like _____

_____

_____

_____

_____

I don't like _____

_____

_____

My First Christmas

was at _____

Other people there _____

_____

_____

_____

My presents _____

_____

_____

_____

Photographs

My First Vacation

was at _____

Date _____

The weather was _____

Other people there _____

_____

_____

Comments _____

_____

_____

Photographs

My First Birthday

I live at _____

My height is _____ Weight _____

My presents _____

_____

_____

_____

_____

_____

_____

My Party

Date _____

Where held _____

Friends and relations there _____

_____

_____

_____

_____

_____

_____

Photographs

Clothes

The first time I dressed myself _____

_____

I wore _____

My favorite dress-ups _____

_____

I won't wear _____

_____

Comments _____

_____

Photographs

Favorites

Music _____

_____

_____

_____

Rhymes _____

_____

Clothes _____

_____

Animals _____

_____

Activities _____

_____

_____

Television Programs _____

_____

I really don't like _____

_____

_____

_____

Best Friends

One Year

photo

Two Years

photo

Comments

Three Years

photo

Four Years

photo

Five Years

photo

Comments _____

_____

_____

_____

_____

My Second Birthday

I live at _____

My height is _____ Weight _____

My presents _____

_____

_____

_____

_____

_____

_____

My Party

Date _____

Where held _____

Friends and relations there _____

_____

_____

_____

_____

_____

_____

Photographs

My Third Birthday

I live at _____

My height is _____ Weight _____

My presents _____

_____

_____

_____

_____

_____

_____

My Party

Date _____

Where held _____

Friends and relations there _____

_____

_____

_____

_____

_____

_____

Photographs

My Fourth Birthday

I live at _____

My height is _____ Weight _____

My presents _____

_____

_____

_____

_____

_____

_____

My Party

Date _____

Where held _____

Friends and relations there _____

_____

_____

_____

_____

_____

_____

_____

Preschool

I started on _____

at _____

My friends are _____

_____

Comments _____

_____

_____

_____

_____

Photographs

Photographs

My Fifth Birthday

I live at _____

My height is _____ Weight _____

My presents _____

_____

_____

_____

_____

_____

_____

My Party

Date _____

Where held _____

Friends and relations there _____

_____

_____

_____

_____

_____

_____

Photographs

Kindergarten

My first day of kindergarten was on _____

at _____

My teacher is _____

Comments _____

_____

_____

_____

_____

_____

Photographs

Drawings

Writing

I could recite the alphabet _____

_____

I started to write _____

I began to read _____

My writing _____

_____

_____

_____

_____

Z Z
Z

Health

Immunization

Age	Vaccine	Date given

*Allergies*_____

_____

_____

*Illnesses*_____

_____

_____

*Comments*_____

_____

_____

My Height

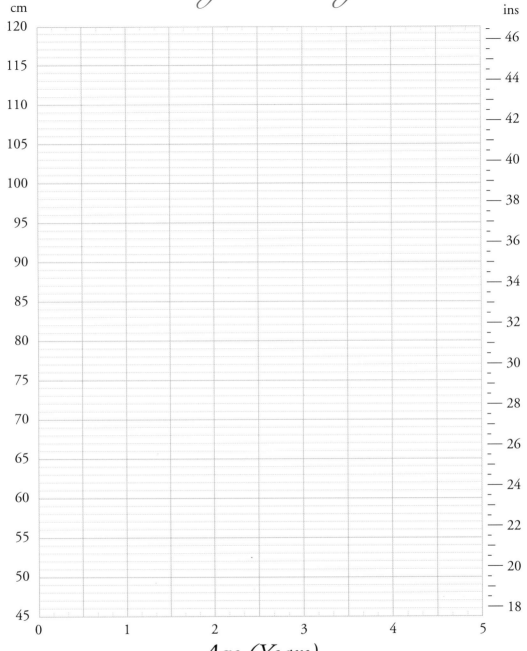

cm / ins — Age (Years)

My Weight

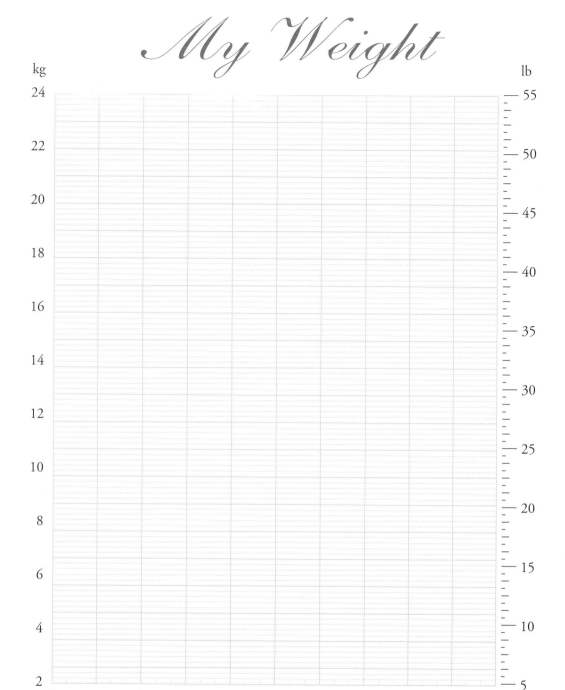

kg   lb

Age (Years)

71

My Teeth

Upper Jaw

Date

8
9
16
13
24

Months

24
13
16
10
7

Date

Lower Jaw

Visits to the dentist

72

The Tooth Fairy's Page

I lost my first tooth on _____

My second tooth _____

The Tooth Fairy left me _____

_____

_____

Comments _____

_____

_____

_____

My Handprints

At birth

At five years

My Footprints

At birth

At five years

Star Signs

Capricorn

22 December – 20 January
Resourceful, self-sufficient, responsible

Aquarius

21 January – 18 February
Great caring for others, very emotional
under cool exterior

Pisces

19 February – 19 March
Imaginative, sympathetic, tolerant

Aries

20 March – 20 April
Brave, courageous, energetic, loyal

Taurus

21 April – 21 May
Sensible, love peace and stability

Gemini

22 May – 21 June
Unpredictable, lively, charming, witty

Cancer

22 June – 22 July
Love security, comfort

Leo

23 July – 23 August
Idealistic, romantic, honorable, loyal

Virgo

24 August – 23 September
Shy, sensitive, value knowledge

Libra

24 September – 23 October
Diplomat, full of charm and style

Scorpio

24 October – 22 November
Compassionate, proud, determined

Sagittarius

23 November – 21 December
Bold, impulsive, seek adventure

Birthstones

January	Garnet – Constancy and truth
February	Amethyst – Sincerity, humility
March	Aquamarine – Courage and energy
April	Diamond – Innocence, success
May	Emerald – Tranquillity
June	Pearl – Precious, pristine
July	Ruby – Freedom from care, chastity
August	Moonstone – Joy
September	Sapphire – Hope, chastity
October	Opal – Reflects every mood
November	Topaz – Fidelity, loyalty
December	Turquoise – Love and success

Flowers

January	Snowdrop – Pure and gentle
February	Carnation – Bold and brave
March	Violet – Modest
April	Lily – Virtuous
May	Hawthorn – Bright and hopeful
June	Rose – Beautiful
July	Daisy – Wide-eyed and innocent
August	Poppy – Peaceful
September	Morning Glory – Easily contented
October	Cosmos – Ambitious
November	Chrysanthemum – Sassy and cheerful
December	Holly – Full of foresight

Comments _____

_____

_____

_____

_____

_____

_____

_____

Photographs

Comments _____

_____

_____

_____

_____

_____

_____

_____

_____

Photographs